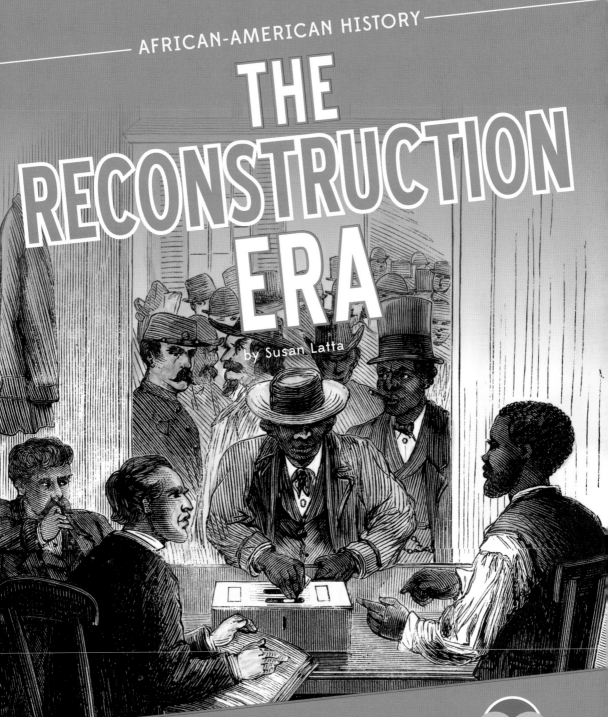

THE RECONSTRUCTION ERA

by Susan Latta

Content Consultant
Ibram X. Kendi, PhD
Assistant Professor, Africana Studies Department
University at Albany, SUNY

Core Library

An Imprint of Abdo Publishing
www.abdopublishing.com

Published by Abdo Publishing, a division of ABDO, PO Box 398166, Minneapolis, Minnesota 55439. Copyright © 2015 by Abdo Consulting Group, Inc. International copyrights reserved in all countries. No part of this book may be reproduced in any form without written permission from the publisher. Core Library™ is a trademark and logo of Abdo Publishing.

Printed in the United States of America,
North Mankato, Minnesota
022014
092014

Editor: Holly Saari
Series Designer: Becky Daum

Library of Congress Cataloging-in-Publication Data
Latta, Susan M.
  The Reconstruction Era / Susan M. Latta.
      pages cm. -- (African-American History)
  ISBN 978-1-62403-147-2
1. African Americans--History--1863-1877--Juvenile literature.
2. Reconstruction (U.S. history, 1865-1877)--Juvenile literature.
3. Southern States--Race relations--History--19th century--Juvenile
literature. I. Title.
  E185.2.L33 2014
  973.8--dc23
                              2013027635

Photo Credits: North Wind Picture Archives via AP Images, cover, 1; North Wind/North Wind Picture Archives, 4, 6, 12, 14, 18, 20, 22, 25, 26, 28, 30, 32, 34, 39, 41, 45; Red Line Editorial, 8, 37; Anthony Berger/Library of Congress, 9; Library of Congress, 16

CONTENTS

CHAPTER ONE

A NEW ERA

In 1619 slavery began in the British colonies in the present-day United States. Africans were brought there against their will. They were forced to work in the fields to grow crops such as tobacco and cotton. They were not paid. They were property of their masters. Many slaves were treated cruelly. They were often whipped and beaten for rebelling.

Slaves could be sold away from their families at any time.

Sometimes dozens of slaves worked on a single plantation in the South.

Slavery in the North and South

In 1783 the United States won its independence from Great Britain. In 1787 the US Constitution was written to govern the new country. Some of the nation's founders did not want slavery to be a part of the country. But most did. Slavery was not outlawed in the document. Each state was able to decide if it wanted to have slavery.

Many Northern states passed laws that would gradually end slavery. But Southern states did not. Most slaves worked in the South on farms or large plantations. Plantation owners depended on the free labor the slaves provided.

As the United States gained new territories in the West, the North and South disagreed on slavery. Some in the North thought new territories should not allow slavery. The South thought slavery should be allowed in the new areas.

Frederick Douglass

Frederick Douglass was an African-American leader of the antislavery movement. He believed the Civil War was a turning point for African Americans. He pressured President Abraham Lincoln on emancipation. He also wanted African Americans allowed to be soldiers. Once Reconstruction began in 1865, he fought hard for African-American rights by making speeches and writing newspaper articles.

The Civil War

The slavery debate brought tension to the country. In 1861 several Southern states left the United States.

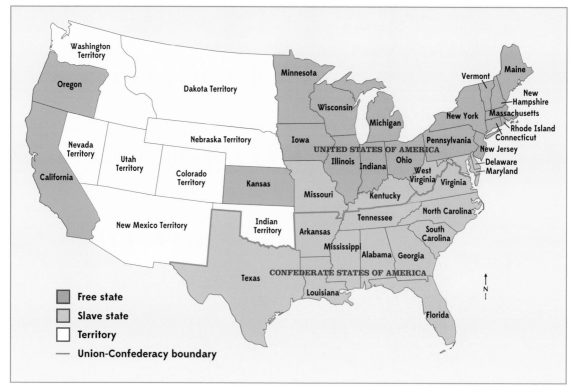

A Country Divided

This map shows the United States in 1861, when the Civil War began. How does seeing free states and slave states help you better understand the Civil War? Does seeing the territories where slavery could have expanded help you better understand reasons for the Civil War? How so?

They formed the Confederate States of America, or the Confederacy. In April 1861, the American Civil War began between the Confederacy and the United States, or Union. The Southern states thought their rights were being taken away. They wanted to decide

Lincoln did not want slavery extended into western territories.

the issue of slavery themselves. They did not want the federal government to decide for them.

The Emancipation Proclamation

While the Civil War was being fought, President Abraham Lincoln formed a plan to reunite the United States and the Confederacy. This plan was called Reconstruction. Its goal was to rebuild the nation after the Civil War.

One of the first stepping-stones to Reconstruction was the Emancipation Proclamation. Lincoln issued the order in 1862. The Emancipation Proclamation stated all slaves living in the Confederacy were free as of January 1, 1863. But Lincoln's order did not do much. The Confederacy was no longer a part of the United States. The proclamation was important though. It changed the course of the war. The Emancipation Proclamation led to many more African Americans serving in the Union army. The Union won the Civil War in April 1865.

Slavery Ends

In December 1865, the Thirteenth Amendment was added to the Constitution. It abolished slavery in the United States. Slaves were now free. They became known as freedmen. But the amendment was only the beginning of what was needed to help the former slaves start their new lives.

US Army chaplain Henry M. Turner was one of many African Americans who celebrated the Emancipation Proclamation. He described the joyful scene when the document was first printed in newspapers:

> Men squealed, women fainted, dogs barked, white and colored people shook hands, songs were sung, cannons began to fire at the navy-yard, and follow in the wake of the roar that had for some time been going on behind the White House. . . . Great processions of colored and white men marched to and fro and congratulated President Lincoln on his proclamation. . . . Nothing like it will ever be seen again in this life."

> Source: Margaret E. Wagner, Gary W. Gallagher, and Paul Finkelman, eds. The Library of Congress Civil War Desk Reference. New York: Simon & Schuster, 2002. Print. 713.

Nice View

After reading Turner's quote, go back and read the section of this book that describes the proclamation. What is the point of view of the book's author? What is Turner's point of view? Write a short essay comparing the two points of view reflected in the main text and in this primary source.

CHAPTER TWO

FREE BUT FEW RIGHTS

When the Civil War ended in 1865, the Reconstruction era began. Once free, former slaves faced many challenges. They had no jobs. They had no land. And they had no place to live. One purpose of Reconstruction was to aid the freedmen in starting their new lives.

Former slaves had to find jobs and homes once they were free.

Some African Americans were given their own land.

Land Given to Freedmen

Former slaves wanted to earn their own livings. Many wanted to work for themselves on their own land. In 1865 African Americans were allowed to apply for land in the South. Most of the land had been abandoned or taken during the war. The land was given to African Americans so they could have their own farms. More than 40,000 former slaves settled on land stretching from South Carolina to northern Florida. But by the middle of 1866, half of this land had been returned to its original white owners.

The Freedmen's Bureau

In 1865 Lincoln created the Freedmen's Bureau. The organization was formed to transition the South from a place of slavery to a place of freedom. The Bureau helped the freedmen find jobs. It helped provide medical care. The Bureau trained new teachers to educate African Americans. A good education was important for freedmen to begin their new lives. The Bureau helped build more than 1,000 schools. African

Sharecropping

African Americans who did not have their own land turned to sharecropping. Sharecroppers worked and lived on land owned by whites. The sharecroppers received a share of the harvested crop. Some African Americans were able to make a meager living this way. But many struggled to get by.

The Freedmen's Bureau helped solve disputes between African-American workers and white landowners.

Americans learned math and English. They were also taught about their culture.

The Black Codes

In April 1865, President Abraham Lincoln was assassinated. Andrew Johnson became president of the United States. Johnson was a southerner. He believed African Americans were inferior to whites.

He did not think they should have the same rights that whites had. The president was no longer working for African-American equality.

At the time, many other whites in the South felt similar to Johnson. They did not like Reconstruction's goals. In 1865 southern states started creating black codes. These were rules and laws meant to limit the rights of African Americans. The black codes limited African Americans' rights to own land and weapons. Some black codes stated the kind of work African Americans could do. Usually this meant working in a field or being a servant. Both were very low-paying jobs.

Radical Republicans

The group in government that most disagreed with Johnson's views was the Radical Republicans. The Radical Republicans believed freedmen deserved civil rights. They made it so Congress controlled Reconstruction rather than the president. This allowed them to continue to work for African-American rights without the president's help.

African Americans often received the most difficult jobs for the lowest pay.

In Mississippi African Americans had to show a written contract proving they had a place to work. If they did not have a job or left their jobs without

FURTHER EVIDENCE

Chapter Two discusses the Freedmen's Bureau. It also discusses education for newly freed slaves in the South. What was one of the chapter's main points? What are some pieces of evidence in the chapter that support this main point? Check out the website at the link below. Does the information on this website support the main point in this chapter? Write a few sentences using new information from the website as evidence to support the main point in this chapter.

Reconstruction: The Second Civil War

www.mycorelibrary.com/reconstruction-era

permission, they could be arrested. The black codes also called for segregation. These rules were the beginning of decades of segregation of African Americans in the South.

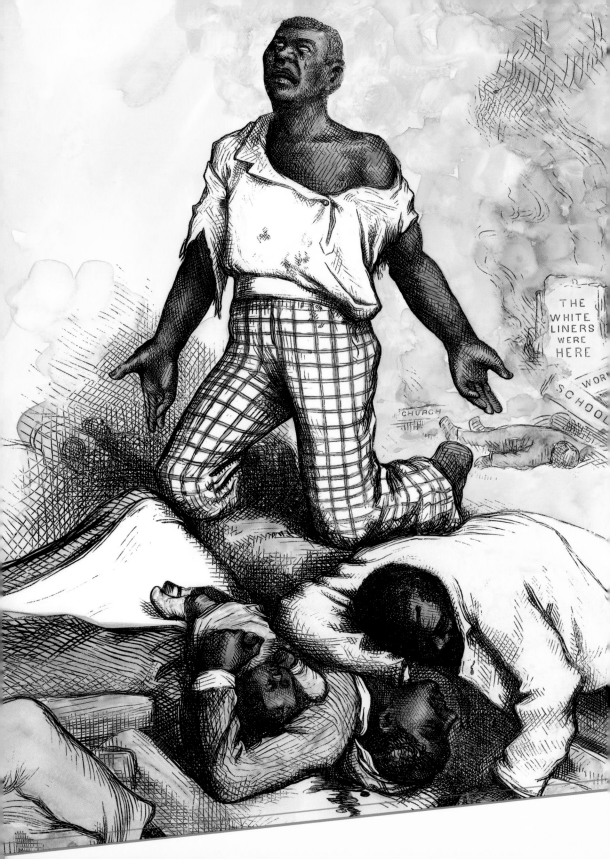

CHAPTER THREE

THE VIOLENT SOUTH

Southern whites did not just pass laws that limited African Americans' rights. They also organized violent acts against African Americans. These acts were meant to intimidate and threaten them. Southern whites even lynched, or hung, African Americans. Usually African Americans had done nothing wrong. White gangs tore through Memphis, Tennessee, in 1866. They killed 46 African Americans.

Some whites set fire to African Americans' homes and property.

Thaddeus Stevens was a Radical Republican who believed African Americans should be treated equally.

The whites also damaged African-American property, including homes, schools, and churches.

Laws to Stop the Violence

Many voters in the North and some in the South were sympathetic to the freedmen. They wanted the violence to stop. Johnson's approach of letting the South control how African Americans were treated was not working. In 1866 many Republicans were elected to Congress. This group believed African Americans should be treated equally. The Republicans helped pass laws hoping to stop the violence. But many of these laws were not strong enough to end it.

The Ku Klux Klan

One of the most violent white gangs was the Ku Klux Klan (KKK). It began in Tennessee around 1866. It soon spread throughout the South. At one time its membership neared 500,000. Its members did not want African Americans to have any rights.

Hiding to Frighten

KKK members dressed in white garments and hoods. They appeared ghostlike when they frightened African Americans. Wearing hoods was also a way to hide their identities. But interviews with freedmen later proved African Americans often knew members of the KKK and who their attackers were.

The KKK wanted to restore the white-controlled South. The KKK's goal was to ruin Reconstruction policies and the Republican Party. The KKK terrorized African Americans and the Republican leaders who worked to give African Americans rights. They worked in small, disguised groups to burn churches and schools. They traveled through the southern countryside to hurt and murder African Americans.

Trying to Fight Back

Republican Party leaders had trouble fighting the KKK. Witnesses to the KKK's actions were often too afraid to testify against the group. If the KKK was charged with a crime, juries made up of racist whites found KKK members not guilty. One way African Americans tried to fight the KKK was through armed self-defense groups. But the KKK proved more powerful than these African-American groups. The KKK killed 20,000 men, women, and children between 1868 and 1871.

KKK members hid their faces with white hoods.

Even after the KKK began to decline, African Americans still faced violence in the South.

The Ku Klux Klan Act of 1871 was passed to punish KKK members who performed violent or illegal acts. In 1872 Klan membership began to decline. But violence against African Americans continued.

African Americans were afraid for their lives, families, and homes because of the KKK. Many experienced the violence firsthand. African-American Simeon Young described what it was like to have the KKK terrorize his home on May 25, 1871:

> On Sunday morning last between 1 and 2 o'clock my wife woke me up, saying there was Ku-Klux outside. I jumped out of my bed and took my rifle. They broke in the window of the bedroom and threw a turpentine ball into the room which I smothered with a blanket. They then went to the front door, burst that in and threw several turpentine balls into the room and then burst open the bedroom door and fired some ten or twelve shots, wounding my wife and child as they lay in bed. I fired upon the nearest man, wounding him. I then jumped through the window and as I was running through the crowd I received two shots in the thigh.

Source: Dorothy Sterling, ed. The Trouble They Seen: Black People Tell the Story of Reconstruction. *Garden City, New York: Doubleday, 1976. Print. 371.*

What's the Big Idea?

Take a close look at this passage. What is Young's main point about life during the KKK's time in power? Pick out two details he uses to make this point. What can you tell about the daily lives of African Americans during this time?

CHAPTER FOUR

RECONSTRUCTION LEGISLATION

A main goal of the Reconstruction era was to make sure African Americans had rights. Legislation was passed to make these rights the law. The first main Reconstruction legislation was the Civil Rights Act of 1866. This act stated all people born in the United States, except Native Americans, were citizens. It gave African Americans the right to make contracts and own property. Under this act,

African Americans gained new rights and opportunities during Reconstruction.

The Civil Rights Act of 1866 gave African Americans the rights of citizens.

African Americans had the right to take part in legal actions, such as lawsuits. The Civil Rights Act of 1866 also made it illegal for the states to pass more black codes.

The Reconstruction Act of 1867

The Reconstruction Act of 1867 stated men of any race could vote. It also allowed a military presence to be set up in the South. Thousands of federal troops were sent to the South to maintain order and protect African Americans from violence. The troops helped oversee voting as well.

The Fourteenth Amendment

In 1868 the Fourteenth Amendment was added to the US Constitution. The amendment guaranteed citizenship to all people born in the United States, with the exception of Native Americans. The amendment was stronger than the Civil Rights Act of 1866. Now individual states could not pass their own laws to override this citizenship rule.

But in 1873 the Supreme Court looked at part of the Fourteenth Amendment. It determined the civil rights granted by the amendment could still be controlled by the individual states.

Challenges of Voting

Most African Americans voted for those in the Republican Party. For a time, Republicans were able to control state governments in the South. This helped African Americans achieve greater equality with whites. But southern whites soon intimidated African Americans into voting for their Democratic candidates. Democrats believed African Americans were inferior. Once the Republicans lost control in the South, African-American rights weakened.

African-American men gained the right to vote in 1870.

This allowed southern states to again limit the rights of African Americans.

The Fifteenth Amendment

The Fifteenth Amendment became part of the Constitution in 1870. It gave African-American men the right to vote. This amendment was stronger than the Reconstruction Act of 1867. No state government could deny voting on the basis of race.

The amendment should have been a huge victory for African Americans. They would now have a larger

EXPLORE ONLINE

The focus in Chapter Four is on the legislation that was passed during the Reconstruction era. The website below discusses the Fifteenth Amendment. As you know, every source is different. How is the information given in the website different from the information in this chapter? What information is the same? How do the two sources present information differently? What can you learn from this website?

Passage of the Fifteenth Amendment
www.mycorelibrary.com/reconstruction-era

say in government because they could help elect its leaders. But voting did not automatically become easy for African Americans. White groups, such as the KKK, used violence and intimidation near voting locations. They hoped to prevent African Americans from voting. Or they forced African Americans to vote for their candidate. So the Fifteenth Amendment did not bring true equality in voting for African Americans.

CHAPTER FIVE

THE END OF RECONSTRUCTION

After the Fourteenth and Fifteenth Amendments passed, African Americans began to be elected to state and national legislatures. They worked to improve public education for African Americans. They established hospitals and orphanages. They also worked for equal access to public transportation and hotels.

African Americans served in government positions during Reconstruction.

African Americans in Congress

Hiram Revels, Joseph Rainey, and Jefferson Long became the first three African Americans to serve in the US Congress. Revels was a Senator. Rainey and Long were in the House of Representatives. The three served from 1869 to 1871. Five African Americans were elected into the 42nd Congress from 1871 to 1873. However, whites by far made up the majority of Congress.

When Reconstruction ended in 1877, 18 African Americans had served in state positions. These included governor and secretary of state. More than 600 African Americans were seated in state legislatures. No African Americans held a major office during Reconstruction in Alabama, Georgia, North Carolina, Texas, or Virginia.

Troops Pulled Out

In 1876 Republican Rutherford B. Hayes and Democrat Samuel Tilden ran for president. The election was very close. Once the votes were counted, the winner was still unclear. Each candidate said he

State	Name	Position	Year(s) Served
Florida	Jonathon C. Gibbs	Secretary of State	1868–73
Louisiana	Caesar C. Antoine	Lieutenant Governor	1873–77
Louisiana	P. B. S. Pinchback	Governor	1872–73
Louisiana	P. B. S. Pinchback	Lieutenant Governor	1871–72
Louisiana	Antoine Dubuclet	Treasurer	1868–77
Louisiana	Oscar J. Dunn	Lieutenant Governor	1868–71
Mississippi	Alexander K. Davis	Lieutenant Governor	1874–76
Mississippi	James Hill	Secretary of State	1874–78
Mississippi	M. M. McLeod	Secretary of State	1874
Mississippi	Hannibal C. Carter	Secretary of State	1873
Mississippi	Hiram Revels	Secretary of State	1872–73
Mississippi	James Lynch	Secretary of State	1869–72
South Carolina	Francis L. Cardozo	Treasurer	1873–77
South Carolina	Richard H. Gleaves	Lieutenant Governor	1873–77
South Carolina	Henry E. Hayne	Secretary of State	1873–77
South Carolina	Alonzo J. Ransier	Lieutenant Governor	1871–73
South Carolina	Francis L. Cardozo	Secretary of State	1868–73

Southern African-American Politicians

The chart above shows information about the few African Americans who served in state offices during Reconstruction. What can you tell about these states? How does this help you understand the information you read in the text?

had won. War talk between the North and the South surfaced once again because they couldn't agree on the election results.

The Democrats' main desire was to regain control of the South. They wanted the Republicans' Reconstruction policies to end. A compromise was reached. It was known as the Compromise of 1877. Hayes would become president. But Democratic governors would be put in charge of southern states. Additionally, federal troops would be removed from the South. When Hayes pulled the last federal troops from Louisiana and South Carolina in 1877, Reconstruction officially ended.

Losing Rights

As the troops marched out, African Americans lost the help they needed to protect their rights in the South. Democrat-controlled states began passing more policies that took African-American rights away. Some states demanded a poll tax. It needed to be paid before any man could vote. African Americans often could not afford these taxes, so they could not vote.

Fewer African Americans were elected to office. George H. White was elected to Congress in 1897.

Once Democrats gained control of the South, African Americans began losing their rights.

Pinckney B. S. Pinchback

Pinckney B. S. Pinchback was the first African-American governor in the United States. He was a Union officer during the Civil War. He first served in public office in the Louisiana State Senate. In 1871 he served as the state's lieutenant governor. In December 1872, he served as governor for five weeks when the current governor was forced to leave office. Another African American would not serve as any state governor until 1989.

He served until 1901. After White, African Americans were not elected to Congress for almost 30 years.

Gains and Failures

One of the biggest gains for African Americans during the Reconstruction era was an increase in public education. Higher education was also expanded. African-American colleges were founded. These included Howard University, Fisk University, and Alcorn State University.

Still most people believe Reconstruction was a failure. The program was meant to help African

Improved education for African Americans was one success of Reconstruction.

Americans gain rights and freedoms in the South. It did for a while. But at Reconstruction's end, southern leaders and governments were taking these rights away. These states passed laws that increased the segregation of African Americans. These policies remained in place until the 1950s and 1960s when the civil rights movement worked to change this.

1863

The Emancipation Proclamation goes into effect.

1865

The Civil War ends. The Reconstruction era begins.

1865

The Thirteenth Amendment abolishes slavery.

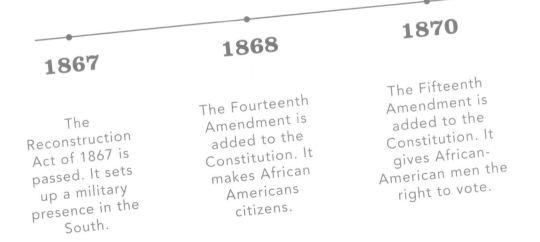

1867

The Reconstruction Act of 1867 is passed. It sets up a military presence in the South.

1868

The Fourteenth Amendment is added to the Constitution. It makes African Americans citizens.

1870

The Fifteenth Amendment is added to the Constitution. It gives African-American men the right to vote.

1865

The Freedmen's Bureau is created.

1865

President Abraham Lincoln is assassinated.

1866

The Civil Rights Act of 1866 is passed, giving African Americans citizenship.

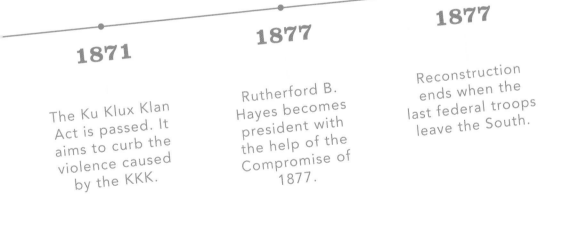

1871

The Ku Klux Klan Act is passed. It aims to curb the violence caused by the KKK.

1877

Rutherford B. Hayes becomes president with the help of the Compromise of 1877.

1877

Reconstruction ends when the last federal troops leave the South.

STOP AND THINK

Take a Stand

Chapter Five discusses the Compromise of 1877. Do you think the Republicans made the right choice when they agreed to take the remaining troops out of the South? Write a short essay explaining your opinion. Make sure to give reasons for your opinion and to support those reasons with facts and details.

Say What?

Studying African-American history can mean learning a lot of new vocabulary. Find five words in this book that you have never heard before. Use a dictionary to find out what they mean. Then write the meanings in your own words, and use each word in a new sentence.

Surprise Me

Chapter Three discusses the violence in the South during Reconstruction. What two or three things surprised you about the Ku Klux Klan? Why did you find them surprising? Write two or three sentences about each.

Another View

Most historians believe Reconstruction was a failure. But some people believe it was a success in some ways. Ask an adult to help you find other sources on this period. Compare and contrast this new source to this book. What are the points of view of the authors? How are they different or similar?

GLOSSARY

abolish
to officially put an end to something

amendment
an addition or change made to an existing law or legal document

bureau
a government division or unit

civil rights
the rights and freedoms of each citizen of the United States

inferior
lower in quality or status

intimidate
to frighten, especially to make someone do something

legislation
rule or law passed by a governing body

radical
favoring drastic political or social changes

segregate
to involuntarily separate or keep people apart from another group

troops
soldiers

LEARN MORE

Books

Osborne, Linda Barrett. *Traveling the Freedom Road: From Slavery and the Civil War through Reconstruction.* New York: Abrams Books for Young Readers, 2009.

Pierce, Alan. *Reconstruction.* Edina, MN: ABDO, 2005.

Websites

To learn more about African-American History, visit **booklinks.abdopublishing.com**. These links are routinely monitored and updated to provide the most current information available. Visit **www.mycorelibrary.com** for free additional tools for teachers and students.

INDEX

ABOUT THE AUTHOR

Susan Latta is a freelance children's writer with a bachelor of science in journalism and mass communications from Iowa State University and a master of fine arts in writing for children and young adults from Hamline University.